# A Very Sloth Christmas

WRITTEN BY
CATHERINE SELF

ILLUSTRATED BY
HEATHER FOXWOOD

Halo
PUBLISHING
INTERNATIONAL

Halo Publishing International
8000 W Interstate 10, #600
San Antonio, Texas 78230

First Edition, November 2022
Printed in the United States of America
ISBN: 978-1-63765-331-9
Library of Congress Control Number: 2022919797

Halo Publishing International is a self-publishing company that publishes adult fiction and non-fiction, children's literature, self-help, spiritual, and faith-based books. Do you have a book idea you would like us to consider publishing? Please visit www.halopublishing.com for more information.

Author's Dedication

This book is dedicated to the love of my life
Richert Leland Self, an amazing husband and
father to our children Caroline and James-David.

Mary, Our Lady of Fatima, pray for us.
October 1, 2022


Illustrator's Dedication

To my husband, Todd, thank you for your
support and believing in me! And to my children
Peter, Joseph, Todd, and Nicholas, I love you
each as the great gifts that God gave me.

"It's Christmas Eve at the Sloth Family Tree,"
said Old Saint Nick with a smile full of glee.
"A family of eight is waiting for us;
let's sit for a moment to talk and discuss."

"Here's Lucy; here's Bella; here's Susie and Tim,
and John and James right next to Dad Jim.
Last, but not least, is this mom of all six,
who soon will be adding to the glorious mix.
A new baby Sloth is due today!
So let's hurry; let's scurry; let's be on our way!"

Sloth Family

"But first," he said with a slight pause,
"we must find gifts worthy of their oohs and their aahs.
Consider each member of this fine clan,
learn all their names, and develop a game plan

so the gifts that we give will come straight from our heart,
gifts they won't find in just any store cart."

9

"First up is Tim—a busy boy, you see.
He loves to laugh and play and just be free.
His days are too short; there's so much to do.
This family of eight is such a fun crew!
He needs a watch to keep his schedule straight,
so he's always on time and doesn't run late."

"Next is Susie—a very smart girl, indeed.
She loves to sit in her chair with a good book and read.
In this Sloth family, she's the one most reserved;
she speaks with a voice that can hardly be heard.
Susie needs a microphone to be heard in this crowd!"
exclaimed Saint Nick with a voice full and proud.

"Now, let's consider Bella,
a princess in her own right.
She loves to twirl and whirl
to everyone's delight.
Her favorite place is her mother's lap;
she refuses to leave for a nod or a nap.
Bella needs a doll so she can sleep through
the night, to help her sleep soundly
when Mom's out of sight."

"Next is Lucy, who loves to move.
Sitting still and silent just isn't her groove.
At church, there's a scene when she runs out of the pew,
leaving Sophie and Jim asking, 'What'll we do?'
"Beads," said Saint Nick, "might keep her mind busy,
help keep her calm and out of a tizzy."

"Then we have John, a most thoughtful Sloth boy.
He's kind and helpful, yet I don't see much joy.
John's heart seems heavy and a wee bit weary,
as if he's trying to grasp a perplexing theory."
Saint Nick then said with a sigh,
"John needs a mirror right next to his bed,
one with these words inscribed in red:
*I see a smile, and I see me.*
*I see good, and that good is me.*"

"Now, see James; he's the oldest of the six.
He can make anything out of nothing but sticks.
In the dark of the night, he often works late
to finish his craft by some special date.
I know what he needs," said Saint Nick with conviction.
"A lamp to work late without any restriction!"

"And now, the Sloth we await with delight,
the one we hope makes her arrival this night.

I think what she needs is a new baby bed,
a place to sleep and rest her sweet head."

23

After talking about each child and the gifts they'd be given,
Saint Nick stood up and seemed very driven.
As he spoke, you could see the twinkle in his eye,
and the smile on his lips one couldn't deny.
His voice was complete with love and compassion
as he spoke of the parents' gift he soon would fashion.

"Now, Sophie and Jim are the best parents I know,"
said Old Saint Nick with his face all aglow.
"Through the bumps and bruises and little ole cracks,
they laugh, and they love, and they live life to the max."

Despite the chaos and clutter that six can create,
Jim told Sophie, "This'll be great!
One more Sloth in our tree house high above!

One more treasure to teach and to love!
More mouths to feed, this is so true,
but don't worry,
Sophie; we'll just make more stew!"

Saint Nick then said aloud,
"They'll need a bigger pot to feed this large crowd!
One that can hold enough food for nine,
like Sophie's stew that tastes so divine!"

Saint Nick then smiled and looked at his watch
as he told both his elves,
"You're really top-notch!
Let's put away the photos and all of our notes,
grab your boots and your overcoats,
load up the sleigh, and ride along with me.
There's a Sloth family we really must see!"

After each gift was delivered on that special night,

Saint Nick and his elves dashed out of sight!

When morning came, the Sloth family opened their gifts, paper and ribbons all thrown adrift. A new little Sloth was on the scene in Sophie's arms, calm and serene.

"What will they name this new addition?"
the elves asked Saint Nick after they
finished their mission.
Saint Nick's big smile then lit up his face
as he told both the elves, "Her name is…"

"...Grace."

CPSIA information can be obtained
at www.ICGtesting.com
Printed in the USA
LVHW072224110723
752229LV00042B/1532